MW00737467

The
Gen Z
DICTIONARY

First Edition

BY KELLY KING
& 80/20 AGENCY

The Gen Z Dictionary

An imprint of 80/20 Agency, LLC

Copyright © 2020 by Kelly King

All rights reserved. No part of this book may be reproduced, stored in a retrieval system, or transmitted in any form, or by any means, electronic, mechanical, photocopying, recording or otherwise, without written permission, except in the case of brief excerpts in critical reviews or articles.

All inquiries should be addressed to
80/20 Agency, P.O. Box 2718, Bloomington, IN 47402.

www.80-20Agency.com

Designed by
Françoise Gagnier and the 80/20 Agency team

ISBN: 978-1-7351877-0-9

Printed in the United States of America

Praise for The Gen Z Dictionary

"This puts Urban Dictionary to bed. My mother knows too much now, nothing gets past her anymore."

-   Meghan Reddy
    Concerned Daughter

"Not only is this book a ton of fun, it illustrates the importance slang plays in our culture. I hope someone has the foresight to place a copy of this book into a time capsule. Future generations will need this to decode the digital messages they find in their archaeological digs. At some point in time tea... will again just be tea."

-   John Campbell
    Father of 3 Gen Z-ers

"As a baby boomer who works solely with college student Gen Z-ers, this is an amazing resource for me and my entire staff! Thanks to the 80/20 team for putting this together. It has allowed us to connect in creative and clever ways with our students."

-   Maureen Biggers, PhD
    Executive Director, IU Center of Excellence for Women & Technology

HOW IT ALL GOT STARTED...

Remember when you were growing up and heard an adult or teacher say something you didn't understand because they used a word you didn't know? It was frustrating. You wanted to have a strong vocabulary like theirs.

Well, the tables have turned. As a mother, employer and university instructor of Gen Z-ers, I experience that feeling frequently. There are new words and expressions continually coming out of their mouths, and it's impossible to keep up with the lingo.

Having our finger on the pulse of Gen Z—those born between 1997 and 2012—is an integral part of our job at 80/20 Agency. The millennials are now getting "old" and the "Z"s are the up-and-coming market every business wants (and needs) to engage with.

My young staff knew I was on a mission to learn their lingo, so we had a running list of Gen Z vocabulary on a simple spreadsheet. I wanted to be able to claim **"I speak Gen Z."**

Then it dawned on me. I needed a Gen Z Dictionary. And, I already had the ideal team of people to write it. Our research was a great conversation starter as we polled friends and family. "What's your latest slang word?" became one of my favorite questions to ask. From there the words started accumulating and the list grew quickly.

It has been almost a year-long process collecting words, defining them, clarifying their pronunciation, and then creating the most genuine sentence to capture the essence of each word with a little humor, of course.

This has been a very collaborative project with many laughs along the way. But, let me tell you, these Gen Z-ers take their vocabulary seriously and do not want their words used incorrectly. We made many edits to get the *vibe* of each word just right.

Many thanks to Françoise Gagnier, our Creative Director, for her attention to detail on the many revisions, and to the 80/20 team for their input on the vocabulary list and definitions. A special thank you goes to my daughter and son, Taylor and Phillip, who *keep it 100* and teach me something new about Gen Z almost every day.

I hope you enjoy learning these words and have even more fun using them in the real world.

Peace!

Kelly King
Founder & President
80/20 Agency

@ me next time /æt mi nɛkst taym/
> *verb* • encouraging someone to be more direct;
> references tagging someone in a social media post
>
> "@ me next time you make fun of people who listen
> to classical music."

adult /ədəlt/
> *verb* • to perform tasks related to being responsible
> or mature
>
> "I just went to the grocery store and paid my bills, I'm
> really adulting today."

and I oop /ænd ay oop/
> *exclamation* • when someone or something catches
> you off guard; reference to a Jasmine Masters
> YouTube video
>
> "And I oop! I almost ran into that trash can!"

(I'm) baby /ˈīm bebi/
> *adjective* • a statement to say when you're incapable
> of doing something
>
> "Can you lift this sewing machine for me? I'm baby."

bae /bay/
> *noun* • a person's dating partner; acronym for
> "before anyone else"
>
> "I love my bae because he makes tacos for me
> whenever I want."

basic /besɪk/
> *adjective* • average or generic, often describing girls
> only interested in mainstream trends; carries
> negative connotations
>
> "Ugh, Stephanie is so basic. She drinks a Pumpkin
> Spice Latte from Starbucks every day."

beat my face /bit may fes/
> *verb* • to put on makeup

"Wait, Caroline, I've got to go beat my face before we can leave for the party."

bet /bɛt/

exclamation • word of affirmation, slang for "okay" or "sure"

"Hey Jim, we're going to the mall later." "Bet."

big /bɪg/

adjective • a lot of; a word of emphasis

"Jordan makes big money selling brownies to the guys in his fraternity."

bless /blɛs/

exclamation • expression of feeling thankful

"I got home from work and my roommate had cleaned the kitchen—bless."

bless your heart /blɛs yɔr hart/

exclamation • positive sounding, subtle put-down implying naivety or low intelligence

"You think potatoes grow on trees? Oh, bless your heart."

(the) bomb /bam/

noun • something considered excellent

"Your aunt's cookies are always (the) bomb."

bool /bool/

verb • to hang out, relax, or chill with friends

"Do you want to bool later?"

bop /bop/

noun • a very good song

"This song is such a bop."

boujee /buži/

adjective • high-end, pretentious; derived from "bourgeoisie"

"That girl is so boujee. Her custom leather jacket cost $3.8 million."

bot /ˈbot/

    noun • someone who has very little personality

    "She's hot, but she's a bot."

bounce /ˈbau̇n(t)s/

    verb • to leave

    "Darrell just showed up with his cat on a leash again. Let's bounce."

bouta /ˈbouta/

    verb • to be about to do something

    "Bouta tuck my napkin in my lap because I'm a messy eater."

bromance /ˈbrō-ˌman(t)s/

    noun • tight friendship between male friends; portmanteau of the words "bro" and "romance"

    "Their bromance is so cute. They have brunch together every Sunday!"

bruh /bruh/

    exclamation • gender-neutral expression of shock or disbelief, usually in response to a dim-witted statement; "are you serious?"

    "Is the Pope Catholic?" "Bruh."

bug out /bəg awt/

    verb • to freak out in a positive or negative way

    "Have you heard Harry Styles' new song? I'm bugging out over it."

bye, Felicia! /bay fəlišə/

    exclamation • dismissive comment; reference to the 1995 movie Friday

    "You ate my fried pickle chips without asking? Bye, Felicia!"

cancel /kænsəl/

    verb • to dismiss someone/something; to reject an individual or idea

"John likes to put ranch on his pizza. He's cancelled."

can't even /can't ivən/

> *verb* • to not be able to deal with or handle something

"Dude, you asked Daniel on a date after he kissed me? I can't even."

catfish /kætfɪš/

> *verb* • to be tricked into a relationship with a fake online persona

"Katy Perry just asked me out on a date!" "How can you think that's real? You're being catfished!"

clapback /ˈklap-ˌbak/

> *noun* • a response to an insult that's better than the insult

"You're broke." "Well, your mom doesn't love you."

clout /ˈklauṫ/

> *noun* • high social standing or notable influence and power

"He got a lot of clout from winning the annual hacky sack tournament."

clown /ˈklauṅ/

> *verb* • to joke

"I'm just clowning. I don't actually think Pepsi is made with eggs."

clutch /kləč/

> *adjective* • exactly what is needed; perfect

"I just found $20 in my pocket! So clutch!"

cooked /kʊkt/

> *adjective* • in need of rest; tired

"I worked 80 hours this week. I'm cooked."

cop /ˈkäp/

> *verb* • to obtain

"I just copped that new Paul Blart movie on Blu-Ray."

4

cringe /krɪnǰ/

 adjective • very awkward, uncomfortable

 "I just ran into my ex with his new girlfriend. The whole interaction was so cringe."

crossed /krɔst/

 adjective • to be drunk and high at the same time

 "Fam, you were so crossed last night."

darty /darti/

 noun • day party

 "Yo, are you throwing another darty this Saturday?"

(I'm) dead /ˈīm ˈded/

 adjective • a response to something really funny

 "My pal Buster laughed and shot milk out his nose. I'm dead."

 verb • find something unbearably humorous

 "Please stop dancing in such a funny way, I'm dying."

deadass /ˈded ˈæs/

 adverb • seriously, literally

 "She's so oblivious, she deadass reversed her car into the closed garage door."

dime /ˈdaym/

 noun • someone who is very attractive

 "Stacy is a dime!"

do you dirty /ˈdü ˈyü ˈdər-tē/

 verb • to cross someone

 "You did me dirty by telling my girlfriend I had six other girlfriends."

do the most /ˈdü-iŋ the ̱ ˈmōst/

 verb • to do more than necessary; excessive, usually has positive annotations

 "Charlie reads six books a day. He's always doing the most."

dope /ˈdōp/

adjective • cool

"Dave Matthews Band is dope."

drag /dræg/

verb • to insult or roast

"Hate to drag myself but I am a terrible cook."

drip /ˈdrip/

noun • clothing and jewelry

"Look at her necklace! She has amazing drip."

electric /əléktrɪk/

adjective • replacement of the overused "cool"

"Electric shoes, man!"

esketit /esketit/

exclamation • let's get it, usually referring to money; coined by Lil Pump

"Bouta hit the farmer's market, esketit!"

extra /ɛkstrə/

adjective • over the top for no reason

"Can't believe you just vacuumed the curtains. Wow, you're so extra."

fam /ˈfam/

noun • group of close friends; short for "family"

"Hey fam, want to all come over for a potluck?"

feels /ˈfilz/

noun • strong feelings

"Those pics of us from freshman year got me in the feels."

exclamation • when you understand how someone else feels

"I'm literally so bored." "Feels."

ferda /ˈferda/

preposition • doing something to make friends happy; short for "for the boys"

"Drink this entire bottle of ranch dressing ferda!"

finesse /fə-ˈnes/

> *verb* • to swoop in and steal someone from their significant other

> "While you were busy at work, I finessed your girl by telling her you were going nowhere in life."

finna /finna/

> *verb* • going to or intending to do something

> "We finna meet up tonight?"

finsta /ˈfinsta/

> *noun* • alternative Instagram account; sometimes anonymous and usually shares more private information

> "Did you see Isaac's finsta post? He has a mysterious new boyfriend!"

fire /ˈfī(-ə)r/

> *adjective* • amazing, great

> "These Triscuits are fire."

fit /ˈfit/

> *noun* • outfit

> "Her fit is amazing from head to toe!"

flex /ˈfleks/

> *verb* • to show off

> "Every time I talk to Katie, she's always flexing about her summer in the Hamptons."

flop /ˈflap/

> *verb* • when something fails; typically relating to a social media post

> "Bruh, that TikTok better not flop."

FOMO /ˈfō ˈmō/

> *noun* • acronym for "fear of missing out"

> "I don't want to go to the Toyota Summer Sale, but my FOMO is acting up."

fried /frayd/

adjective • crazy

"Your dream about swimming with monkeys was absolutely fried."

full send /fʊl sɛnd/

exclamation • do something without thinking of the consequences

"Should I buy the boat?" "Full send, baby!"

G /ji/

noun • term of endearment between male friends

"You got this, G! You're gonna ace that test."

gas me up /ˈgas ˈmē ˈəp/

exclamation • to give compliments

"You like my ankles? What else do you like? Gas me up, son!"

get crunk /ˈget ˈkrəŋk/

verb • to party hard

"Let's get crunk this weekend. My bar mitzvah will have so much pizza."

get it /ˈget ˈit/

verb • to get after it; to be excited

"Packers' game is about to start. Let's get it."

get this bread /ˈget ˈthis ˈbred/

verb • to make money

"I just sold my toy collection on eBay for a lot of money—I'm getting this bread."

get iced /ˈgɛt ayst/

verb • to come across a Smirnoff Ice purposefully hidden by another person as part of a party game; the discoverer must take a knee and drink the whole beverage immediately

"I just got iced by Trevor hiding a bottle in the microwave for me to find. I chugged the whole thing like a champ."

ghost /ˈgōst/
> *verb* • to suddenly avoid someone or stand them up
> "I asked if she wanted to have a baby, and now she's ghosting me."

glow up /ˈglō ˈəp/
> *noun* • a personal positive transformation over time, especially with concern to looks
> "Sharon has been working out and just bought a new outfit—get ready for her glow up."

GOAT /ˈgōt/
> *noun* • acronym for "greatest of all time"
> "Michael Jordan is the GOAT."

go off /go ɔf/
> *verb* • to encourage someone to keep up what they are saying or doing; building someone up
> "How does this outfit look?" "DAAANG girl, go off!"

gotta blast /ˈgä-tə ˈblast/
> *verb* • to have to leave
> "I gotta blast—the Wiggles is about to start."

the grind /thə ˈgrīnd/
> *noun* • hard work
> "I've been writing this Toy Story fan fiction for thirteen weeks, and it's almost done. I'm on the grind."

gucci /guči/
> *adjective* • good
> "So we're going to the club after we watch Toy Story? Sounds gucci."

high key /ˈhī ˈkē/
> *adverb* • very obvious

"High key, I hate Jessica. Everyone does."

hit different /ˈhit ˈdi-f(ə-)rənt/

verb • to have a novel effect

"Michael Jackson is great, but Thriller hits different after I watched the Netflix documentary about him."

hmu /ˈhmu/

exclamation • acronym for "hit me up"

"I'm so bored right now, hmu."

homie /ˈhō-mē/

noun • a good or close friend

"Ben is always there for me. He's such a homie."

homie hopper /ˈhō-mē ˈhä-pər/

noun • girl who dates multiple guys within a single friend group

"Watch out for Jane. She's a homie hopper. She's dated John, Matt and Chris, and I heard she's into Sam."

hot mess /ˈhät ˈmes/

noun • a person who is not put together

"Your socks don't match today? You're a hot mess."

hot take /ˈhät tek/

noun • a personal opinion; often controversial or unpopular

"I don't think you want to hear my hot take on your new song."

hype /hayp/

verb • positively building someone up about something; encouraging

"I just got my make-up done and my best friend won't stop hyping me up about it."

adjective • exciting or awesome

"I just met Mark Cuban!" "That's hype!"

icymi /áy sí wáy ém áy/

   expression • acronym for "in case you missed it"
   "Here's a link to the meme of the day icymi."

iconic /aɪˈkɒn ɪk/

   adjective • highly influential or unique
   "Beyoncé's album Lemonade is truly iconic."

iykyk /ɪf yu no yu no/

   expression • acronym for "if you know you know"
   "Remember what happened last time I wore this
   shirt?" "Ha...iykyk."

irl /ay ar ɛl/

   preposition • acronym for "in real life"
   "He doesn't have any friends irl. He only talks to
   people online."

it be like that /ɪt bi layk ðæt/

   expression • stating the unfortunate truth
   "I'm on my fifth cup of coffee today. It be like that
   sometimes."

keep it 100 /ˈkēp ˈit ˈwən-ˈhən-drəd/

   verb • to keep it real, to be honest; to do something
   with integrity
   "Tell her you like her! Keep it 100."

(the) lab /thə læb/

   noun • a place you go to improve yourself like a gym
   or library
   "Tanner and I are going to get a quick workout at the
   lab."

lit /ˈlit/

   adjective • really good or fun
   "This pie-baking contest is lit."

look like a snack /luk ˈlīk ˈā ˈsnak/

   verb • to look excellent, attractive

"Dang girl, I like your sundress. You're looking like a snack."

low key /ˈlō ˈkē/
> *adverb* • keep quiet about; often precedes an honest opinion
>
> "I know Lisa is narcissistic but, low key, she is an amazing painter and I wish her well."

major /ˈmā-jər/
> *adverb* • extreme; very
>
> "He tried to drink a gallon of milk before his flight. Major yikes."

make money moves /meɪk məni muvz/
> *verb* • to do big things, especially financially
>
> "I just sold Jordans for double what I paid; I'm making money moves."

me /mi/
> *noun* • slang for "me too" or "I can relate"
>
> "I never remember to bring an extra pair of socks for after my workout." "Me."

meme /mēm/
> *noun* • a humorous, relatable image or video that goes viral
>
> "Whenever I want to relax, I just look through the latest dog memes on Instagram."

(a) mood /ˈmüd/
> *noun* • the feeling of something being relatable
>
> "Did you see that boy crying after he dropped his ice cream cone on the ground? That is a mood."

nice with it /ˈnīs ˈwith ˈit/
> *adjective* • good, smooth; often related to physical activities like basketball
>
> "He's nice with it on the court—he crossed me up and scored."

no cap /ˈnō ˈkap/
    adverb • seriously, literally
    "I ate an entire pizza by myself last night, no cap."
OG /o ˈji/
    noun • acronym for "Original Gangster"; a title
    denoting authenticity and respect; often conveys
    something is "old school"
    "I first learned how to make pasta from my grandma.
    She is the OG pasta maker."
on point /ˈȯn ˈpȯint/
    adjective • perfect; dressed appropriately, in
    regards to style
    "Your outfit is on point today—your belt perfectly
    matches your shoes."
on the dl /ˈan ðə dl/
    prepositional phrase • on the "down low"; keep
    something quiet
    "On the dl, I'm super into him."
on the real /an ðə ril/
    prepositional phrase • emphasizes an honest
    statement
    "On the real, you're the funniest person I've ever
    met."
oof /oof/
    exclamation • slang for "yikes"; acknowledging
    something unfortunate
    "I just killed a huge spider in my room." "Oof."
(we) outtie /ˈwi outie/
    expression • we're leaving
    "This party is lame. I hate Yahtzee. We outtie."
pause /ˈpȯz/
    verb • to tell someone to wait or stop speaking for a
    second

"Pause—did you just say that you wear Wonder Bread
as shoes?"

periodt /ˈpir-ē-əd/

exclamation • emphasis of "this is the truth"

"Girls don't like me. Periodt."

pocket /pakət/

verb • to steal or take suspiciously

"I may have to pocket the last Rice Krispies Treat."

pop-off /pap ɔf/

exclamation • a compliment when someone looks
good or does something impressive

"You look so good in that outfit! Pop-off, sis!"

pwn /ˈpōn/

verb • to outdo or beat someone; used by people
playing video games

"I pwned you in Pokémon so hard."

real one /ˈrē(-ə)l ˈwən/

noun • someone you trust

"Chris is a real one—when I crashed my car, he came
and picked me up on his bike."

receipts /ri-ˈsēts/

noun • proof

"She's cheating on you and I've got receipts to prove
it—look at these text messages."

rents /rɛnts/

noun • short for "parents"

"Sorry I'm late, I just got off a call with the rents."

roast /ri-ˈsēts/

verb • to insult someone

"I can't believe you let him talk bad about you. Aren't
you going to roast him back?"

salty /ˈsȯl-tē/

adjective • bitter, angry

"You're just salty because your parents went to the
   movie without you."

savage /ˈsævɪǰ/

   noun • someone who does not care about the
   consequences of their actions

   "You don't want to make Tony mad; he's a savage."

send it /ˈsend ˈit/

   verb • to go for it; reference to texting

   "Should I eat another bagel?" "Send it!"

ship /ˈship/

   verb • to optimistically imagine two people, often
   fictional characters from a book or television show,
   in a relationship together in your head; derived
   from "relationship"

   "I know he's with Rachel, but I ship James with Jenna.
   They'd be so cute together!"

shook /ˈshuk/

   adjective • rattled; amazed

   "His beautiful voice has me shook."

shots fired /šats fayərd/

   exclamation • response to someone using an insult
   against someone else

   "He just told her she drives like a grandma—shots
   fired!"

shotgun /šatgən/

   verb • to chug a beer through a hole made in the
   side of a beer can

   "Chad's talent is shotgunning beers."

sick /sik/

   adjective • cool

   "Congrats on getting a full-ride to Stanford. That's
   sick!"

simp /ˈsimp/

noun • short for "simpleton"; a guy who does
whatever a girl says to win her over
"Brad does whatever Ashley says. He even washed
her car for her yesterday. He's such a simp."

sis /sɪs/
>*noun* • a term of endearment, usually toward a
>female friend
>"There's no one else quite like you, sis."

sisters /sɪstər/
>*noun* • a close group of friends, usually female
>"Thanks for coming to our first sweet potato club
>meeting, sisters."

sksksk /sksksk/
>*exclamation* • laugh of a VSCO girl (pg. 19) when
>they find something amusing; used ironically
>"I'm only going to get 4 hours of sleep tonight—
>sksksk."

slaps /ˈslaps/
>*verb* • to be good, often referring to songs
>"'All By Myself' by Céline Dion slaps."

smack /ˈsmak/
>*verb* • to eat in abundance or quickly
>"I'm about to smack some fries."

SnapTrap /ˈsnap ˈtrap/
>*noun* • a Snapchat sent to see if someone is ignoring
>your texts
>"She opened my Snapchat, but hasn't responded to
>my text—she fell for my SnapTrap."

snatched /ˈsnached/
>*adjective* • looking good
>"You look snatched in those overalls."

snatch (your) wig /snæč yɔr wɪg/

verb • to expose someone in front of others;
reference to RuPaul's Drag Race

"Somebody is going to snatch your wig if you aren't
honest about how you really feel."

square up /skwɛr əp/

verb • to prepare to fight

"My brother better square up when he realizes I
know he broke my favorite mug."

stan /ˈstan/

noun • die-hard fan; reference to Eminem's song
"Stan"

"I've been a Hunkleberry Funk stan since I heard their
first album."

step off /ˈstep ˈòf/

verb • to back off; to mind your own business

"Step off, dude—stop asking me to share straws."

stonks /ˈstonks/

exclamation • used ironically for small financial gain

"Carl just paid me $5 for my Rolex." "Stonks!"

straight fire /stret fayər/

adjective • something really good or nice

"This new Taylor Swift album is straight fire."

sus /ˈsəs/

adjective • short for "suspicious"; suggests
questionable behavior

"That man looks sus. He's been staring at us all night."

swoll /ˈswoll/

adjective • muscular

"He's swoll now; he does a pull-up a day."

take an L /ˈtāk ən ˈel/

verb • to take a loss

"You told your wife you thought her outfit was ugly?
Guess you took an L there."

tbh /ˈtē ˈbē ˈāch/

    prepositional phrase • acronym for "to be honest"

    "I hate everyone who likes sushi, tbh."

tea /ˈtē/

    noun • gossip

    "I've got some tea to spill—Derek's dad is addicted to IHOP."

(I'm) tee'd /ˈīm ˈtē'd/

    adjective • to be mad; ticked off

    "I'm so tee'd because my pancakes are soggy."

that ain't it /ðæt ent ɪt/

    exclamation • unacceptable; to say that something is a horrible idea

    "You want to eat a burrito and then race a mile? No, that ain't it!"

that's the move /ðæts ðə muv/

    exclamation • a good idea

    "Kinsey recommended going to Chick-fil-A for breakfast—we all know that's the move."

thicc /ˈthic/

    adjective • curvy, often relating to girls

    "That girl is thicc."

thirsty /ˈthər-stē/

    adjective • desperate; usually related to dating

    "That boy from last weekend is so thirsty. He's sent me 187 text messages since then."

throw shade /ˈthrō-iŋ ˈshād/

    verb • to subtly put someone down

    "Quit throwing shade and tell me how you feel!"

tight /ˈtīt/

    adjective • angry, on-edge

    "She said I looked like Michelle Wie and I'm tight."

tmk /tí ém ké/

prepositional phrase • acronym for "to my knowledge"

"Everyone in Hawaii is happy all the time, tmk."

trill /ˈtril/

 adjective • slang for "true" and "real"; authentic

 "The lyrics to that song are trill."

triggered /trɪgərd/

 adjective • upset, sad, disgusted, set off

 "Hearing my ex's favorite song in the Uber had me triggered."

twisted /twɪstəd/

 adjective • to be drunk and high at the same time

 "Fam, you were so twisted last night."

unsult /un-ˈsəlt/

 noun • an insult disguised as a compliment

 "I love how you can just do whatever you want with no repercussions." "Was that an unsult?"

vibe /vayb/

 noun • the energy or mood projected by a person, place or thing; usually positive

 "Our neighbors spend the summer drinking beer and listening to country music on their porch, that's such a vibe."

VSCO girl /visko gərl/

 noun • a stereotype term for teen girls who carefully follow current aesthetic and style trends; trends that are particularly popular on the photo editing app, VSCO.

 "Have you seen all of Becky's new scrunchies? She's such a VSCO girl."

wack /ˈwæk/

 adjective • crazy, weird, unbelievable

"Did you see Chad throw the bookshelf out his window?" "No, that's wack!"

what's good /wäts ˈgu̇d/

> *expression* • slang for "what's up?"
>
> "What's good, Tom? I haven't seen you in like six days!"

wild /wayld/

> *adjective* • eventful behavior or experience; another way of saying "crazy"
>
> "I was not expecting her to have a trampoline in her house. That was wild."

woke /ˈwōk/

> *adjective* • socially conscious
>
> "Thank you for encouraging me to gain awareness of my prejudices. You're so woke."

woof/wu̇f/

> *exclamation* • expression of defeat or tiredness
>
> "It's been a long day...woof."

yeet /ˈyēt/

> *exclamation* • expression of excitement, often said while throwing an object
>
> "Wanna go watch middle school volleyball?" "Yeet."
>
> *verb* • to throw something
>
> "Although he was the last pick, Robbie yeeted the dodgeball right at Kyle and won us the game."

yikes /ˈyīks/

> *exclamation* • bad move
>
> "He's bringing home a kitten even though his roommates are allergic—yikes."

you got jokes /ˈyü gat ˈjōks/

> *expression* • sarcastic response to an insult or diminutive comment

"You think you can beat me one-on-one on the
court? You got jokes."

you're trippin' /yər ˈtrip-iŋ/

  expression • you're crazy; you're wrong

  "You think McDonalds uses horse meat? You're
  trippin'."

zooted /zooted/

  adjective • very intoxicated from drugs and/or
  alcohol

  "I was so zooted yesterday, I don't even remember
  eating that pizza."

Think you know Gen Z?

Download the latest facts on Gen Z at
www.80-20agency.com/genzfacts

What's good, Gen Z?!

Is there a word you use that you don't see in here?

Keep us in the know by submitting your lingo at:
www.TheGenZDictionary.com/pages/submit

We appreciate it, on the real.

Bless,
80/20 Agency

www.TheGenZDictionary.com
email: hey@TheGenZDictionary.com

@genzdictionary

Many Thanks To:

Staff and Interns of 80/20 Agency

Fraternity and Sorority Members at Indiana University

Agency 7 Students at The Media School
at Indiana University

The many Gen Z-ers we randomly asked

www-80-20agency.com

Made in the USA
Middletown, DE
09 December 2023

45122874R00020